WOMEN OF THE BIBLE

The Old Testament

WOMEN OF THE BIBLE

THE OLD TESTAMENT

Written by the
Daughters of St. Paul

Illustrations by Gregori

ST. PAUL EDITIONS

NIHIL OBSTAT:
REV. MSGR. MATTHEW P. STAPLETON

IMPRIMATUR:
✠ HUMBERTO S. MEDEIROS
Archbishop of Boston

November 5, 1970

Library of Congress Catalog Card Number: 71–145574

PRINTED IN THE U.S.A. BY THE DAUGHTERS OF ST. PAUL
50 ST. PAUL'S AVENUE, BOSTON, MASS. 02130

THE DAUGHTERS OF ST. PAUL ARE AN INTERNATIONAL RELIGIOUS CONGREGATION SERVING THE CHURCH WITH THE COMMUNICATIONS MEDIA.

Contents

Introduction

There is an old saying that a woman never goes to heaven alone but always takes at least one man with her—be he husband or son, father, brother or friend. It is of woman's very nature to influence man for good or evil. "No woman can be neutral in the world," wrote a famous educator. "She, too, is set for the fall and for the resurrection of many."

Salvation history, like profane history, bears this out: the Sacred Scriptures present us with such bold contrasts as Phutiphar's wife and Pharao's daughter, Dalila and Ruth, Michol and the mother of the Machabees.

The lessons these lives present for our consideration are now more relevant than ever.

"At this moment," declared the Fathers of the Second Vatican Council, "when the human race is undergoing so deep a transformation, women impregnated with the spirit of the Gospel can do so much to aid mankind in not falling. You women have always had as your lot the protection of the home, the love of beginnings and an understanding of cradles. You are present in the mystery of a life beginning. You offer consolation in the departure of death.

"Our technology runs the risk of becoming inhuman. Reconcile men with life and above all, we beseech you, watch carefully over the future of our race. Hold back the hand of man who, in a moment of folly, might attempt to destroy human civilization."

EVE

MOTHER OF ALL THE LIVING

"Rejoice, O Father Adam, and even more, rejoice and exult, Mother Eve. You, the first parents of all the living, have unfortunately given life to mankind, tainted with sin. But now you can be comforted in your great daughter. O Eve, the shame that you have passed down to all women will now be taken away.

"The time has come when a Woman will take away whatever men may have against women. Once, man crudely tried to blame the woman, actually saying, 'The woman you gave to me, gave me the fruit of the tree, and I ate it.'

"Therefore, O Eve, hasten to Mary. O mother, hasten to your daughter. The daughter will answer for the mother, will take away the cloud. Man fell once through a woman; now he is raised up through a woman.

"What did you say, Adam? 'The woman that you gave me fed me the fruit of the tree.' These were malicious words which only increased your guilt. But wisdom conquered malice and still found a way to show mercy, even after you responded improperly to God's questions. In His wisdom, God found a treasury of pardon.

"A woman is given for a woman, a prudent virgin for a foolish virgin, a humble girl for a proud one. In place of the fruit of death she offers a taste of life. In place of the bread of bitterness, she gives the fruit of eternal life.

"Still those words of malice, Adam, and say gratefully, 'Lord, the woman you gave to me has fed me from the tree of life. It is sweeter than honey; it is life-giving!'" (St. Bernard)

—Genesis 2 and 3

HER SORROW TURNED TO JOY

Sara was the wife of the patriarch Abraham, "Father of All Believers." At the command of God, she journeyed with her husband to the land of Chanaan, which the Lord then promised to Abraham and to his descendants: "All the land which you see I will give to you and your posterity forever...."

Abraham believed the word of the Lord, even though he and his wife were advanced in years. To emphasize Sara's share in the covenant promise, God changed the pronunciation of her name (which means "princess") and said: "I will bless her, and she shall be the mother of nations; kings of peoples shall descend from her." Abraham laughed in surprise.

Sara herself was to react in a similar fashion upon receiving this news. Visitors

came to Abraham's tent and were given refreshment by him in the noonday shade. Gradually these guests revealed their divine mission: "At this time next year, Sara your wife shall have a son." And Sara, who had remained hidden inside the tent, laughed in amazement.

"Why did Sara laugh?" demanded the heavenly messenger. "Why did she say, 'Shall I indeed bear a child, though I am old?' Is anything too wonderful for the Lord?" Thus was emphasized the extraordinary nature of this event. The next year the child was born, and a happy Sara exclaimed: "God has given me cause for laughter." They called him Isaac, a name that echoed their joy, for it means "God has smiled."

Abraham and Sara are both praised for their faith: "By faith he who is called Abraham obeyed by going out into a place which he was to receive for an inheritance; and he went out, not knowing where he was going.... By faith even Sara herself, who was barren, received power for the conception of a child when she was past the time of life, because she believed that He who had given the promise was faithful" (Hebrews 11:8-11).

Because of Sara's constant obedience to her husband, St. Peter considers her a model for wives and mothers: "Let wives be subject to their husbands.... Let not theirs be the outward adornment of braiding the hair, or of wearing gold or of putting on robes; but let it be the inner life of the heart, in the imperishableness of a quiet and gentle spirit, which is of great price in the sight of God. For after this manner in old times the holy women also who hoped in God adorned themselves, being subject to their husbands. So Sara obeyed Abraham, calling him Lord. You are daughters of hers when you do what is right and fear not disturbance" (1 Peter 3:1-6).

—Genesis 13 to 21

Praise of God's Provident Care

Praise, you servants of the Lord,
praise the name of the Lord.
Blessed be the name of the Lord
both now and forever.
From the rising to the setting of the sun
is the name of the Lord to be praised....
He raises up the lowly from the dust;
from the dunghill he lifts up the poor
To seat them with princes,
with the princes of his own people.
He establishes in her home the barren wife
as the joyful mother of children.

—Psalm 112

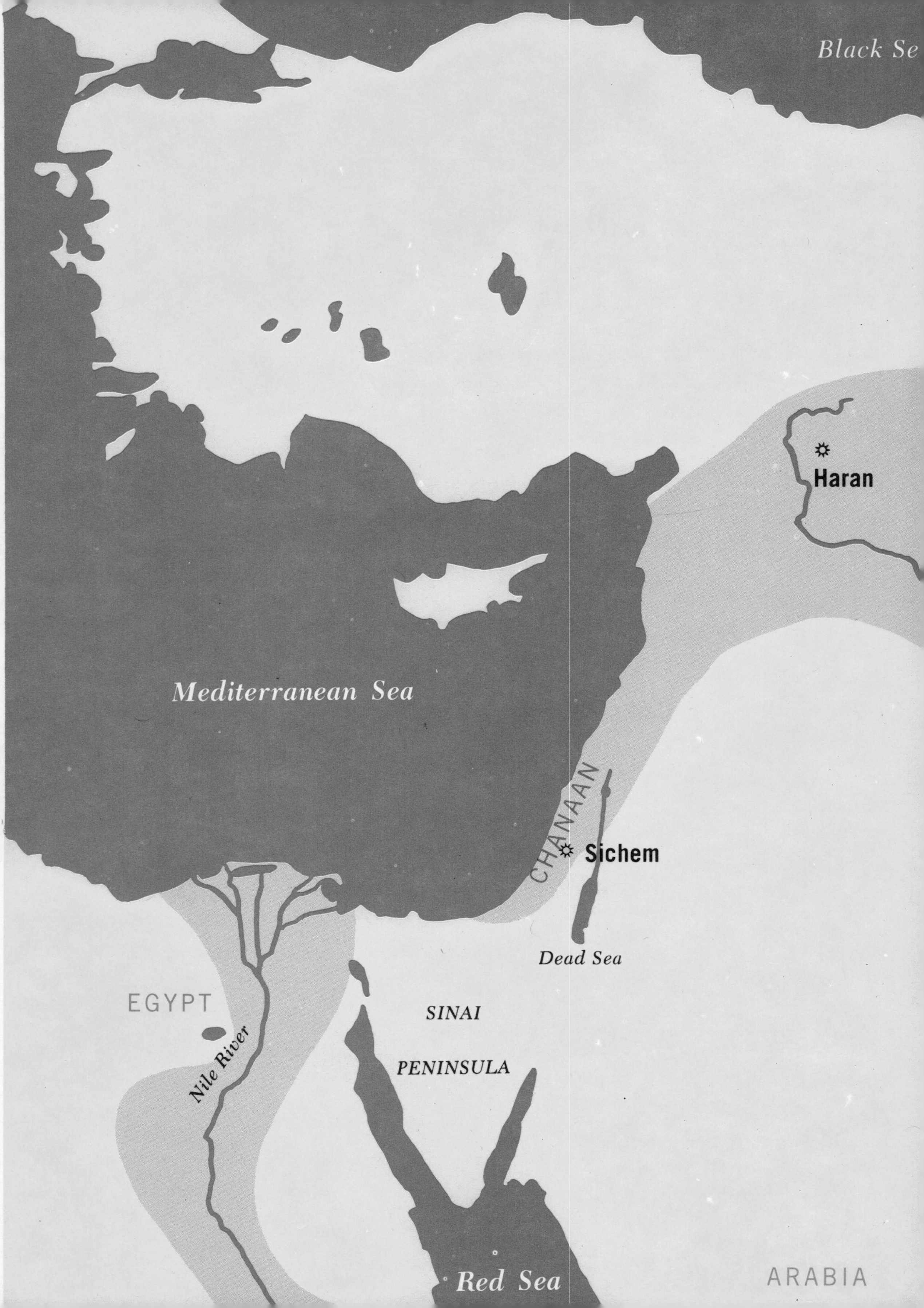

Black Se

Haran

Mediterranean Sea

CHANAAN

Sichem

Dead Sea

EGYPT

SINAI

PENINSULA

Nile River

Red Sea

ARABIA

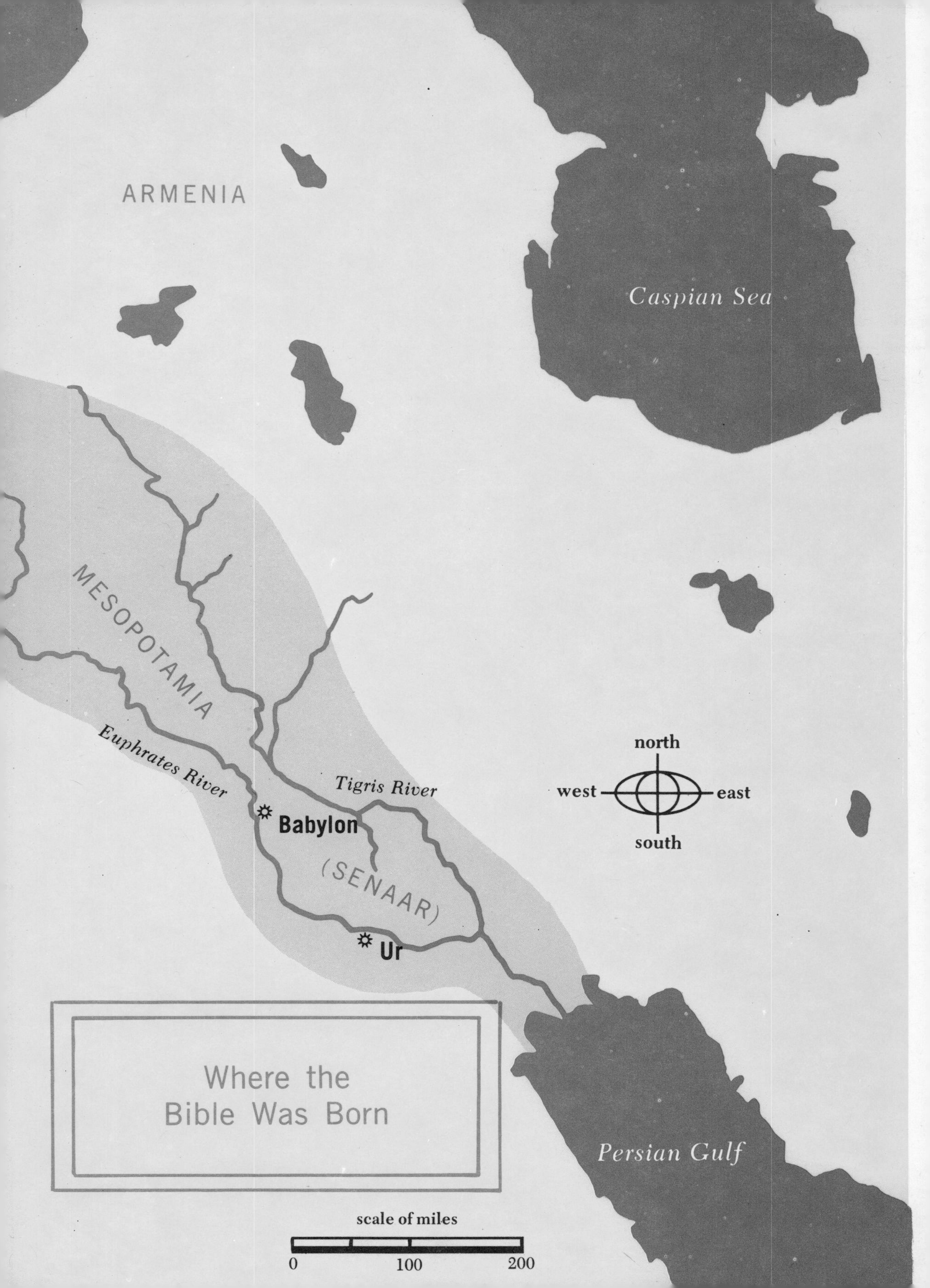
ARMENIA
Caspian Sea
MESOPOTAMIA
Euphrates River
Tigris River
Babylon
(SENAAR)
Ur
north
west
east
south
Where the
Bible Was Born
Persian Gulf
scale of miles
0
100
200

THE LORD HEARD HER PRAYER

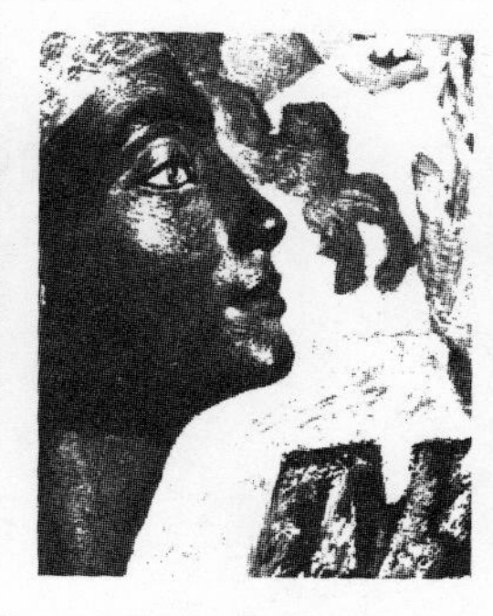

Agar was Abraham's slave and the mother of his firstborn son, Ismael. She was dismissed shortly after Sara bore to Abraham Isaac, the son of the promise.

Abraham gave Agar bread and a bottle of water and dismissed her with her son. She departed and journeyed into the desert. When the water in the bottle was gone, the grieving mother left her child in the shelter of a bush and went apart a short distance. "Let me not see the child die," she prayed. Ismael cried out and God heard the boy's cry.

An angel spoke to Agar: "What is the matter, Agar? Fear not, for God has heard the boy's cry in this plight of his. Rise up, take the boy, be assured in his regard, for I will make him a great nation."

Trusting in God's word and in His providence, Agar looked up and saw a well not far off. She went and filled the bottle with water and gave the boy a drink. They continued their journey into one of the deserts of Sinai, where they settled. Ismael grew up to be the father of a great nation, as had been foretold to his mother.

—Genesis 16 and 21

Hymn of Gratitude

I love the Lord because he has heard
my voice in supplication.
Because he has inclined his ear to me
the day I called.
The cords of death encompassed me;
the snares of the nether world seized upon me;
I fell into distress and sorrow,
And I called upon the name of the Lord,
"O Lord, save my life!"

Gracious is the Lord and just;
yes, our God is merciful.
The Lord keeps the little ones;
I was brought low, and he saved me.
Return, O my soul, to your tranquillity,
for the Lord has been good to you.
For he has freed my soul from death,
my eyes from tears, my feet from stumbling.
I shall walk before the Lord
in the lands of the living.

—Psalm 114

REBECCA

A LINK IN A CHAIN

When Abraham was very old, he called the oldest servant of his household and had him swear an oath not to obtain a wife for Isaac—son of the promise—from among the pagans of Chanaan. "But go to my land and kindred to obtain a wife for my son Isaac," the patriarch commanded.

Accompanied by ten treasure-laden camels, Abraham's servant journeyed to the city of his master's kinsfolk. In the evening, at the time when the women came out to draw water, he made the camels kneel near the well outside the city. Then he said, "Lord, God of my master Abraham, grant me success this day; be gracious to my master Abraham. I stand here at the spring, and the young women of the city are coming out to draw water. Now if I say to a young woman,

‘Lower your jar that I may drink,’ and she answers, ‘Drink, and I will also water your camels,’ she it is whom You have chosen for Your servant Isaac. Thereby shall I know that You have shown Your favor to my master.”

He had not yet finished speaking when Rebecca came out from the city with a jar on her shoulder. The young woman was very beautiful, a virgin undefiled. She went down to the spring and filled her jar. As she came up, the servant hastened to meet her and said, “If you please, let me drink a little water from your jar.” She answered, “Drink, sir,” and quickly lowered the jar and gave him a drink. Then she said, “I will draw water also for your camels until they have finished drinking.” She quickly emptied her jar into the trough, hastened again to the well, and drew water for all the camels.

Upon learning that Rebecca was Abraham’s kinswoman, the servant went to see her family. He told them of his master’s wishes and the way in which God had answered his prayer. Her family replied, “This comes from the Lord. Let Rebecca be married to your master’s son as the Lord has decided.”

Willingly Rebecca accompanied the servant to the land of Chanaan, where she was married to Isaac. Thereafter she conceived the twins, Esau and Jacob, the younger of whom God chose to inherit the promises made to Abraham.

—Genesis 24 and 25

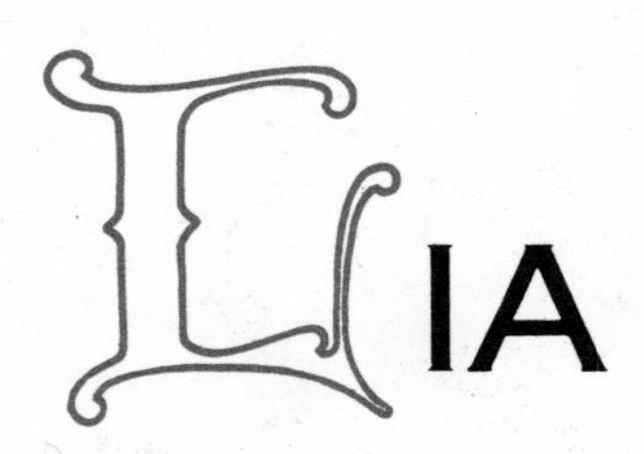

IA

STEADFAST AND LOYAL

To Jacob, younger son of Isaac and Rebecca, God renewed the promise He had made to Abraham: "You shall spread abroad to the west, to the east, to the north, and to the south; in you and in your descendants all the nations of the earth shall be blessed."

Jacob was sent by his father to choose a wife from among the daughters of his kinsman, Laban. "Laban had two daughters," states the Holy Bible. "The elder was called Lia, and the younger Rachel. Lia's eyes were weak, but Rachel was shapely and beautiful."

Jacob served Laban seven years for his younger daughter, Rachel, only to be tricked by his kinsman into marrying Lia instead. Then, in accord with ancient oriental

custom, he was permitted to marry Rachel also, on the condition that he serve Laban another seven years. This Jacob did.

The story of Lia cannot be separated from that of her sister, Rachel, for a strong rivalry sprang up between them. "When the Lord saw that Lia was disliked, He made her fruitful, while Rachel remained barren...." Only after Lia had borne Jacob several children, did God grant fecundity to Rachel also.

Lia appears to have been a woman of fidelity and self-sacrifice, whom God watched over mercifully and made an instrument in the fulfillment of His mysterious designs for the prophetic destiny of the chosen people. Fully half of the tribes of the chosen people trace their ancestry directly to Lia. These include the priestly tribe of Levi, whose greatest representatives were to be Moses and Aaron, and the royal tribe of Juda, whose greatest representative was to be Jesus Christ Himself, the Savior of the world.

—Genesis 29 and 30

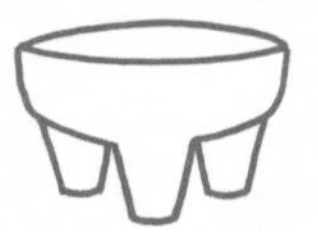

The Need of God's Blessing—
His Gift of Sons

Unless the Lord build the house,
they labor in vain who build it.
Unless the Lord guard the city,
in vain does the guard keep vigil.
It is vain for you to rise early,
or put off your rest,
You that eat hard-earned bread,
for he gives to his beloved in sleep.

Behold, sons are a gift from the Lord;
the fruit of the womb is a reward.
Like arrows in the hand of a warrior
are the sons of one's youth....

Happy are you who fear the Lord,
who walk in his ways!
For you shall eat the fruit of your handiwork;
happy shall you be, and favored.
Your wife shall be like a fruitful vine
in the recesses of your home;
Your children like olive plants
around your table.
Behold, thus is the man blessed
who fears the Lord....

My son, forget not my teaching,
keep in mind my commands;
for many days,
and years of life, and peace,
will they bring you.
Let not kindness and fidelity leave you;
bind them around your neck;
then will you win favor and good esteem
before God and man.
Trust in the Lord
with all your heart,
on your own intelligence rely not;
in all your ways
be mindful of him,
and he will make straight your paths.
Be not wise in your own eyes,
fear the Lord
and turn away from evil;
this will mean
health for your flesh
and vigor for your bones.
Honor the Lord with your wealth,
with first fruits
of all your produce.

—Psalms 126 and 127; Proverbs 3

RACHEL

SWEET AND GENTLE

Jacob, heir of the promises made by God to Abraham, had two wives, in accord with the custom of his times.

It was Rachel whom Jacob met first, and it was for her hand that he asked. The Book of Genesis tells us that upon his arrival in Phaddan-Aram, the land of his kinsmen, Jacob approached some shepherds gathered about a stone-covered well and asked about his uncle – Laban, son of Nahor. "Is he well?" Jacob asked. "He is," they replied, "and here comes his daughter Rachel with his flock."

"While he was still talking with them, Rachel arrived with her father's flock; for it was her custom to tend them. When Jacob saw Rachel, the daughter of his uncle Laban, with the flock, he drew near, rolled the stone from the mouth of the well, and watered his uncle's flock. Then Jacob kissed Rachel and wept aloud. He told Rachel that he was her father's relative, a son of Rebecca, and she hastened to tell her father....

"Jacob loved Rachel. He said, therefore, 'I will serve you seven years for your younger daughter Rachel.' Laban answered, 'It is better to give her to you than to another man; stay with me.' So Jacob served seven years for Rachel, and they seemed to him but a few days because of his love for her."

Lia bore Jacob several children, but it was only after long years of waiting that God heard Rachel's prayer and made her fruitful. The child was Joseph—that pure and just young man through whom God would providentially lead His people down into Egypt where they would grow into a great nation.

Rachel named her second son Benoni—"my sorrow"—for he was born on her deathbed upon the return of Jacob and his family to the land of Chanaan. Jacob, deeply saddened at her death, but happy to have another son—a pledge from God for the future—changed the child's name to Benjamin.

Rachel was buried in Rama, not far from Bethlehem. Years later the prophet Jeremia was to say: "A voice was heard in Rama, weeping and loud lamentation; Rachel weeping for her children, and she would not be comforted, because they are no more." St. Matthew applied this prophecy to the slaughter of the holy Innocents during the fruitless attempt of Herod the Great to kill the infant Christ, the Savior of the world.

—Genesis 29 to 35

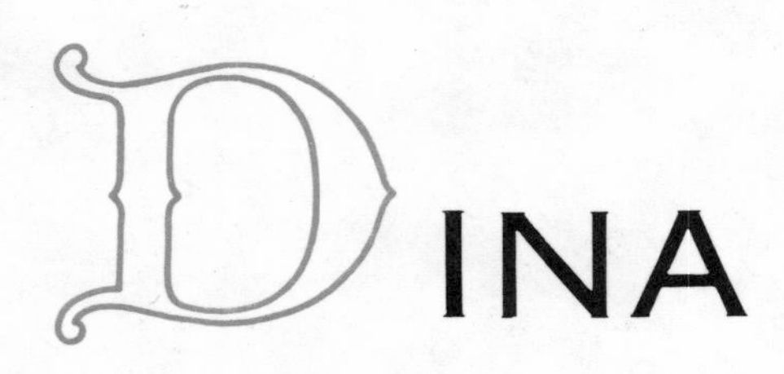

DINA

VICTIM OF DISHONOR

Dina was the only daughter of the patriarch Jacob. When she was about twelve or thirteen, she went to visit the pagan women of the region through which her family was traveling. The occasion may have been some celebration. However, Dina paid a high price for her curiosity. One of the princes of the region committed an outrage against her.

The girl's brothers immediately avenged the crime. Even though their action was cruel and bloody, this shows us how highly woman's honor was valued, even in those primitive and savage times.

In his Epistle to the Romans, the Apostle Paul says: "Do you not know that all we who have been baptized into Christ Jesus have been baptized into his death? For we were buried with him by means of Baptism into death, in order that, just as Christ has arisen from the dead through the glory of the Father, so we also may walk in newness of life.

"For if we have been united with him in the likeness of his death, we shall be so in the likeness of his resurrection also. For we know that our old self has been crucified with him, in order that the body of sin may be destroyed, that we may no longer be slaves to sin; for he who is dead is acquitted of sin. But if we have died with Christ, we believe that we shall also live together with Christ; for we know that Christ, having risen from the dead, dies now no more, death shall no longer have dominion over him. For the death that he died, he died to sin once for all, but the life that he lives, he lives unto God. Thus do you consider yourselves as dead to sin, but alive to God in Christ Jesus.

"Therefore do not let sin reign in your mortal body so that you obey its lusts. And do not yield your members to sin as weapons of iniquity, but present yourselves to God as those who have come to life from the dead and your members as weapons of justice for God" (Romans 6:3-13).

—Genesis 34

PHUTIPHAR'S WIFE

AN INSTRUMENT OF PROVIDENCE

"For those who love God, all things work together unto good" (Romans 8:28).

These inspired words of the Apostle Paul are well illustrated by the history of Joseph in Egypt.

The Book of Genesis relates: "When Joseph was taken down in Egypt, Phutiphar, an Egyptian, one of Pharao's officers, the captain of his bodyguard, bought him from the Ismaelites who had taken him down there.... When his master saw that the Lord was with him and prospered all his undertakings, Joseph found favor with him and became his attendant. He placed him in charge of his household and entrusted all his property to him."

Joseph was good-looking, however, and his master's wife repeatedly endeavored

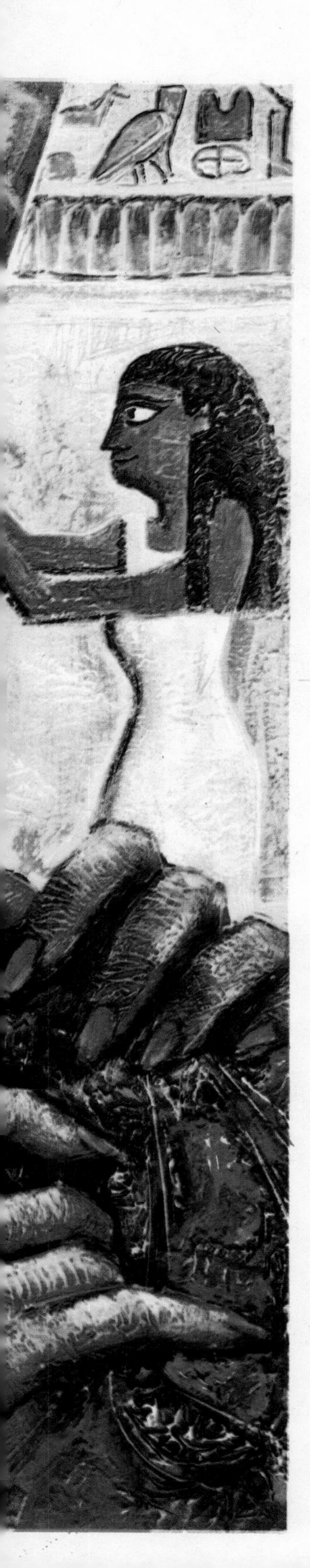

to tempt him to sin. Each time, the God-fearing young Hebrew refused. "How can I commit such a great crime and sin against God?" he asked.

Finally the woman accused Joseph to her husband—accused him of the very sin he had hotly refused to commit. She was believed, and the handsome young Hebrew was thrown into prison.

The rest of the story of Joseph is known to all. He interpreted Pharao's dream and became viceroy of all Egypt. Declares the Book of Wisdom: "Wisdom did not abandon the just man when he was sold, but delivered him from sin. She (Wisdom) went down with him into the dungeon, and did not desert him in his bonds, until she brought him the scepter of royalty and authority over his oppressors, showed those who had defamed him false, and gave him eternal glory" (Wisdom 10:13-14).

The wife of Phutiphar—her very name is unknown to us—disappears from the pages of Scripture after a very brief mention. If she ever repented and asked forgiveness, we can imagine Joseph addressing to her the same words of trust in Divine Providence that he addressed to those brothers of his who had sold him into slavery in the first place: "You intended evil against me, but God intended it for good...namely, to save the lives of many people."

—Genesis 39 to 50

Security under God's Protection

You who dwell in the shelter of the Most High,
who abide in the shadow of the Almighty,
Say to the Lord, "My refuge and my fortress,
my God, in whom I trust."
For he will rescue you from the snare of the fowler,
from the destroying pestilence.
With his pinions he will cover you,
and under his wings you shall take refuge;
his faithfulness is a buckler and a shield.
You shall not fear the terror of the night
nor the arrow that flies by day;
Not the pestilence that roams in darkness
nor the devastating plague at noon.
Though a thousand fall at your side,
ten thousand at your right side,
near you it shall not come.
Rather with your eyes shall you behold
and see the requital of the wicked,
Because you have the Lord for your refuge;
you have made the Most High your stronghold.

No evil shall befall you,
nor shall affliction come near your tent,
For to his angels he has given command about you,
that they guard you in all your ways.
Upon their hands they shall bear you up,
lest you dash your foot against a stone.
You shall tread upon the asp and the viper;
you shall trample down the lion and the dragon.

Because he clings to me, I will deliver him;
I will set him on high
because he acknowledges my name.
He shall call upon me,
and I will answer him;
I will be with him in distress;
I will deliver him and glorify him;
with length of days I will gratify him
and will show him my salvation.

—Psalm 90

SEPHRA AND PHUA

THEY LOVED LIFE

The providence of God had brought Jacob, his sons and grandchildren into Egypt, where the Israelites rapidly grew in numbers, as the Lord had promised Abraham: "I will indeed bless you, and will surely multiply your descendants as the stars of the heavens, as the sands of the seashore" (Genesis 22:17).

One of the pharaos became alarmed. "Look how numerous and powerful the Israelite people are growing," he exclaimed, "more so than we ourselves! Come, let us deal shrewdly with them to stop their increase; otherwise, in time of war they too may join our enemies to fight against us."

Pharao reduced the Israelites to slavery, and set them to making mortar and bricks and building cities. Yet the more the Hebrews were oppressed, the more they multiplied.

Then pharao called Sephra and Phua, who acted as midwives for the Hebrew women, ordering them to kill every Hebrew baby boy as soon as he was born. "The midwives, however, feared God; they did not do as the king of Egypt had ordered them, but let the boys live."

"The midwives feared God." We do not know if these good women were Hebrews or Egyptians (in Hebrew, "Sephra" means beauty and "Phua" means brightness, but these may nonetheless be derivations of Egyptian names). What we do know is that Sephra and Phua were obedient to the natural law written in their hearts by God. They lived by that great truth which the Second Vatican Council expressed in these words: "God, the Lord of life, has conferred on men the surpassing ministry of safeguarding life..." (Church in the Modern World, n. 51).

The true beauty and brightness of Sephra and Phua were pleasing to the Lord, and the Book of Exodus concludes the episode with the words "God dealt well with the midwives...."

—Exodus 1

PHARAO'S DAUGHTER

WARM WAS HER HEART

Thanks to the God-fearing midwives, Sephra and Phua, the Hebrews in Egypt continued to increase in number. As a result, the fearful pharao commanded all his subjects, "Throw into the river every boy that is born to the Hebrews, but you may let all the girls live."

Not long after this, a boy was born to a Hebrew couple of the tribe of Levi. Strong in her faith, the child's mother hid him for three months. Then she placed him in a papyrus chest made watertight with bitumen and pitch and set it among the reeds at the riverbank, at the spot where Pharao's daughter usually came to bathe. The child's sister waited nearby, so as to offer to provide a nurse for him.

The princess arrived, emerging from obscurity to take her place in the history of salvation. She spied the chest and sent her maids to fetch it. As the good Hebrew mother had hoped, the wailing infant moved Pharao's daughter to pity. She knew at once who the child was: "It is one of the Hebrews' children!" But this did not deter her from saving him. She asked "one of the Hebrew women"—the boy's own mother—to nurse him, and then took him into her own household. That she provided him with a good education and position may be known from Acts 7:22: "Moses was instructed in all the wisdom of the Egyptians and was mighty in words and deeds."

Nothing further is known of this compassionate, courageous Egyptian princess. But her warmheartedness and respect for human life have not been forgotten, for they have been given an enduring monument in the revealed Word of God.

—Exodus 1 and 2

MIRIAM

SHE SANG OF LIBERATION

Miriam, sister of Moses and Aaron, is regarded as one of the many Old Testament types of Mary, Mother of Christ. Favored by God with the gift of prophecy, Miriám broke into a song of exultation after the Israelite passage through the Red Sea, just as Mary most holy, upon being acknowledged as Mother of the Messia, sang a canticle of thanksgiving for the new liberation and redemption.

The canticle of Miriam is regarded by many as one of the most ancient pieces of Hebrew poetry. At once lyric and epic, it vibrantly expresses enthusiasm for the goodness and power of God, who had granted a gratuitous, total and absolute exaltation of the just over the unjust: "Sing to the Lord for he is gloriously triumphant; horse and chariot he has cast into the sea...." (Exodus 15:21)

But even God's favored ones may turn away from Him, as Miriam did when she influenced Aaron to complain against Moses. The humble and God-fearing Moses, "by far the meekest man on the face of the earth" (Numbers 12:3), suffered the disturbance in silence, whereupon the Lord Himself moved in to chastise Miriam, afflicting her with white leprosy, the mildest form of that dread disease. Miriam and Aaron repented and begged forgiveness; Moses prayed to the Lord for his sister. After Miriam had done seven days' penance, the disease left her and she was welcomed back into the ranks of the Hebrews, who had postponed their departure from Sinai until her restoration.

This incident in the life of one of God's favored ones clearly illustrates the necessity of repentance and satisfaction for sin.

—Exodus 15 and Numbers 12

DEBORA

SHE SANG OF TRIUMPH

Often in the course of salvation history, God chose a woman to reawaken the religious consciousness of Israel. One of the greatest of these women was Debora, the prophetess, who lived during the stormy period of the Judges and was herself a "judge," that is, a leader and liberator of her people.

When the Hebrews were sorely oppressed by a powerful Chanaanite king, Debora sent for the general Barak and urged him to join battle with the foe. As a sign of divine backing, the Israelite commander was ordered to descend from Mt. Tabor and meet the better-equipped enemy on an equal footing in the middle of the Plain of Esdraelon.

Barak's swift victory was immortalized in the canticle of Debora, one of the most

ancient and brilliant of all Old Testament canticles. It has all the color and vibrancy of a minor Illiad....

"I to the Lord will sing my song, my hymn to the Lord, the God of Israel.... The kings came and fought; then they fought, those kings of Chanaan, at Thaanach by the waters of Mageddo; no silver booty did they take. From the heavens the stars, too, fought; from their courses they fought against Sisara. The Wadi Kishon swept them away.... Then the hoofs of the horses pounded, with the dashing, dashing of his steeds.... May all your enemies perish thus, O Lord! but your friends be as the sun rising in its might!"

Indomitable and exquisitely poetic, Debora re-kindled the religious-political consciousness of the Hebrews and helped them regain a sense of unity and national tradition sorely needed during the transitional era of the Judges.

—Judges 4-5

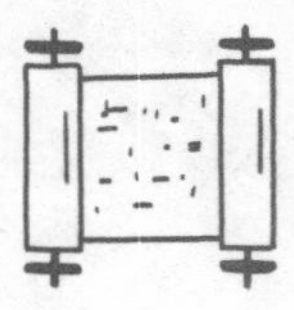

THE HOLY LAND

LAND AT OR BELOW SEA LEVEL

LOWLAND PLAINS

LOW HILL COUNTRY

HILLS AND MOUNTAINS

LEBANON MOUNTAINS

MT. HERMON

GALILEE

Sea of Galilee

o MT. CARMEL

River Yarmuk

Nazareth

o MT. THABOR

DECAPOLIS

PLAIN OF ESDRAELON

o MT. GILBOA

PLAIN OF SHARON

(FORESTED MOUNTAINS)

o MT. EBAL

River Jabbok

o MT. GERIZIM

SAMARIA

River Jordan

PEREA

Mediterranean Sea (The Great Sea)

PHILISTINE PLAIN

SHEPHELAH (FOOTHILLS)

JUDEA

Jerusalem

o MT. NEBO

Bethlehem

JUDEAN HILL COUNTRY

(DESERT)

Dead (Salt) Sea

Canyon of Zered

NEGEB PLATEAU

ARABAH VALLEY

MT. SEIR

north

west

east

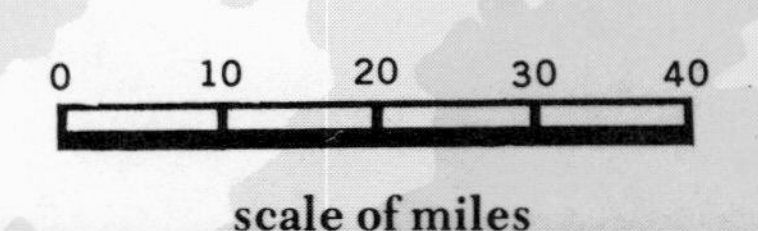

JEPHTE'S DAUGHTER

JOY BECAME MOURNING

The Book of Judges does not tell us the name of this brave teenager, the only child of a fierce Israelite chieftain.

Jephte was God-fearing, but had only an imperfect understanding of the divine will. Before joining battle with his enemy he vowed: "Whoever comes out of the doors of my house to meet me when I return in triumph from the Ammonites shall belong to the Lord. I shall offer him up as a holocaust."

And God granted the victory.

Upon Jephte's return to his house, he was met by a band of women who were celebrating his triumph. His only daughter led them, playing tambourines and dancing for joy. "Alas, daughter," exclaimed the anguished father, "you have struck me down and brought calamity upon me! For I have made a vow to the Lord and I cannot retract." His conscience being but imperfectly formed, Jephte did not realize that the sacrifice of human victims, so common in his day, was neither demanded nor approved by God—the sole Master of life.

The girl's response was truly heroic: "Father, you have made a vow to the Lord. Do with me as you have vowed, because the Lord has wrought vengeance for you on your enemies." She then asked leave to spend two months mourning her virginity—for to die without posterity was a real tragedy to the peoples of that era. It was only in New Testament times that virginity consecrated to God came to be recognized as a state of great nobility: "The virgin thinks about the things of the Lord, that she may be holy in body and in spirit. Whereas she who is married thinks about the things of the world, how she may please her husband" (1 Cor. 7:34).

At the end of the mourning period, Jephte's daughter presented herself to her father, "who did to her as he had vowed."

—Judges 11

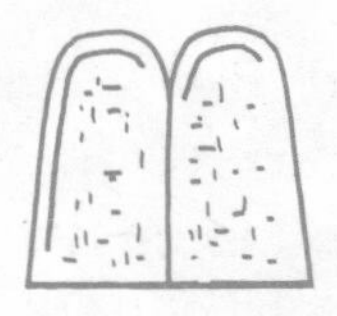

DALILA

SHE ACHIEVED HER GOAL

Samson, son of a devout Israelite couple, had been consecrated to God from birth. He was the terror of the enemy Philistines, for the spirit of the Lord was upon him and he was strong and fearless.

Determined to overcome Samson, the Philistine leaders approached their countrywoman, Dalila, for they knew that the Hebrew giant had fallen in love with her. "Find out the secret of his great strength," they urged, "and how we may overcome and bind him so as to keep him helpless." And perhaps from motives of patriotism or perhaps because she had been offered several thousand silver shekels, Dalila set about wheedling from Samson the secret of his strength.

He told her first one tale, then another. But Dalila was not easily defeated. "How

can you say you love me," she pouted, "when you do not confide in me? Three times already you have mocked me, and not told me the secret of your great strength." She coaxed and complained until Samson grew "deathly weary" and told her the truth: he had been consecrated to God by vow. No razor had ever touched his head, for as a Nazorite he did not cut his hair. "If I am shaved," he explained, "my strength will leave me and I shall be as weak as any other man."

And so it was. While Samson slept, Dalila had his head shaved. He awoke to find himself powerless against the Philistines, who seized and blinded him and took him off to make sport of him.

Sorrowful and repentant, the blinded Samson was led to stand between the two central columns that supported the roof of the temple of Dagon. Three thousand Philistine men and women waited for him to entertain them. "O Lord God," the Hebrew warrior prayed, "remember me! Strengthen me, O God!" and the Lord heard his prayer. Samson braced himself between the columns and pushed until the entire roof of the temple collapsed, killing them all.

Was Dalila there? We do not know. With Samson's capture she disappears from the pages of the Book of Judges, yet not without leaving us another striking example of woman's immense power—a power that can lead man toward, or away from, his God.

—Judges 13 to 16

DALILA — SHE ACHIEVED HER GOAL

RUTH

"YOUR PEOPLE WILL BE MY PEOPLE"

Centuries of oral and written transmission and translation have never lessened the simple freshness of the story of Ruth.

The biblical account opens with a touching scene that took place some three thousand years ago on the sun-drenched plateau of Moab, east of the Dead Sea. Noemi, a Hebrew widow, was about to return to her homeland. Her Moabite daughters-in-law, also widows, asked to accompany her. They felt they owed much to this gentle woman who had no one left in the world.

"Go back, my daughters," Noemi urged. "Go, each of you, to your mother's house." At first neither would depart, but at last Orpha gave in and tearfully said good-bye.

Ruth, however, could not bear to leave Noemi. "Do not ask me to abandon or forsake you," she pleaded. "For wherever you go, I will go; wherever you lodge I will lodge; your people shall be my people, and your God my God...."

Thus, Ruth accompanied Noemi to Bethlehem. They found the fields gold with the harvest and, according to the custom of the times, Ruth set about supporting her mother-in-law by gathering up grain left behind by the reapers in the fields. From the very beginning, everyone noticed that she worked from morning to evening without sparing herself. Soon, too, the whole region knew of her filial devotion to Noemi.

Such love and fidelity did not go unrewarded, just as they would not in our own day. The fruit of Ruth's goodness was her very happy marriage to Noemi's kinsman, Booz. To them was born a son, Obed, the joy of Noemi's old age, who became the grandfather of David. Thus, the gentle Ruth entered into the world's greatest ancestral line—that of David and of Jesus Christ.

—Ruth 1 to 4

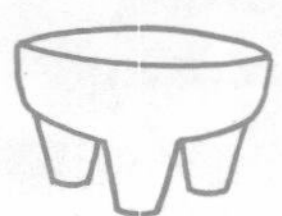

6. Women of the Bible (O.T.)

The Ideal Wife

When one finds a worthy wife,
her value is far beyond pearls.
Her husband,
entrusting his heart to her,
has an unfailing prize.
She brings him good, and not evil,
all the days of her life.
She obtains wool and flax
and makes cloth with skillful hands.
Like merchant ships,
she secures her provisions from afar.
She rises while it is still night,
and distributes food to her household.
She picks out a field to purchase;
out of her earnings she plants a vineyard.
She is girt about with strength,
and sturdy are her arms.
She enjoys the success of her dealings;
at night her lamp is undimmed.
She puts her hands to the distaff,
and her fingers ply the spindle.
She reaches out her hands to the poor,
and extends her arms to the needy.

She fears not the snow for her household;
all her charges are doubly clothed.
She makes her own coverlets;
fine linen and purple are her clothing.
Her husband is prominent at the city gates
as he sits with the elders of the land.
She makes garments and sells them,
and stocks the merchants with belts.
She is clothed with strength and dignity,
and she laughs at the days to come.
She opens her mouth in wisdom,
and on her tongue is kindly counsel.
She watches the conduct of her household,
and eats not her food in idleness.
Her children rise up and praise her;
her husband, too, extols her:
"Many are the women of proven worth,
but you have excelled them all."
Charm is deceptive and beauty fleeting;
the woman who fears the Lord is to be praised.
Give her a reward of her labors,
and let her works praise her
at the city gates. —Proverbs 31

ANNA

SHE ASKED OF THE LORD

From all over Israel pilgrims had thronged to the shrine at Silo, abode of the Ark of God. It was the season to offer sacrifice to the Lord.

Among the pilgrims were Elcana of the tribe of Ephraim and Anna his wife. After the offering of the sacrifice, Elcana brought Anna the customary portion; she, however, burst into tears. Her sorrows had mounted for some time, and now not even her husband's tender concern could restore calm.

One only could check her tears, and Anna hastened off to pray before the Lord. To Him she poured out the misery of her childlessness. "O Lord of hosts," she vowed, "if you look down on the affliction of your servant, and will give your servant a man child, I will give him to the Lord all the days of his life."

Sensitive to the worth and wonder of life and to the true dignity of womankind, this devout Hebrew begged the Lord for a priceless gift. And when He responded by sending her a son, Anna sang a hymn of praise that pealed down the ages—a canticle which so caught the spirit of Yahweh's poor ones that the Virgin Mary herself wove phrase after phrase of it into her matchless Magnificat.

The child Samuel, whose name means "asked of God," grew up to be a true spiritual leader in Israel.

And Anna's faith and gratitude were further rewarded when the Lord sent her three more sons and two daughters.

May such simple reverence for life as hers live on in our world of tension and turmoil, to draw down upon us all the blessings of God.

—1 Samuel 1 and 2

HER PRIDE WAS HER DOWNFALL

The fortune of Michol, daughter of King Saul, rose and fell during the years of turmoil that ushered in Israel's golden age. At first, life held only the brightest prospects. She was a daughter of a king and the wife of the king's bravest captain—David, whom the Israelite women welcomed home from battle with timbrels and cornets as they sang, "Saul has slain his thousands and David his ten thousands."

The wrath of a jealous Saul, however, soon drove David into hiding, and Michol, after helping him escape, found herself waiting anxiously for...she knew not what. Then word came of David's marriage to Abigail, and Saul gave Michol in marriage to Phaltiel of Gallium.

After death put an end to Saul's frantic attempts to preserve the kingdom for himself and his sons, David sent for Michol and took her into his harem.

But Michol's rise in fortune was brief. Looking out her window one day, she saw David leaping and dancing before the ark of the Lord as it was being carried into the city, and in her heart she despised the king. She met him as he came to bless the house and told him he had made a fool of himself.

"Before the Lord," retorted David, "who chose me rather than your father,...I will both play and make myself meaner than I have done, and I will be little in my own eyes!"

For her lack of reverence, Michol received the greatest punishment that could befall a woman of the nation that awaited the Messia: "therefore Michol the daughter of Saul had no child to the day of her death."

—1 and 2 Samuel

Canticle of David

Blessed are you,
O Lord the God of Israel,
our father from eternity to eternity.
Yours, O Lord, is magnificence, and power,
and glory, and victory;
and to you is praise;
for all that is in heaven,
and in earth,
is yours;
yours is the kingdom, O Lord,
and you are above all princes.
Yours are riches,
and yours is glory;
you have domination over all;
in your hand is power and might;
in your hand greatness
and the empire of all things.
Now therefore, our God,
we give thanks to you,
and we praise your glorious name.
Who am I,
and what is my people,
that we should be able to promise you
all these things?

All things are yours
and we have given you
what we received of your hand.
For we are sojourners before you,
and strangers,
as were all our families.
Our days upon earth
are as a shadow,
and there is no stay....

I know my God that you prove hearts,
and love simplicity,
wherefore I also
in the simplicity of my heart
have joyfully offered all these things;
and I have seen with great joy
your people, which are here present,
offer you their offerings.
O Lord God of Abraham,
and of Isaac,
and of Israel
our fathers,
keep forever this will of their heart.

—1 Chronicles 29

ABIGAIL

THE PEACEMAKER

David, son of Jesse, and his fighting men were in hiding. In order to escape the insane jealousy of King Saul, they fled through the barren hill country of Juda, moving from cave to cave. At one point their provisions ran out completely, and it was then that David thought of Nabal, a wealthy sheep-owner whose herdsmen he had often protected in the desert.

The bad-tempered Nabal greeted David's envoys with an insult.

"Gird on your swords!" David told his followers when he heard this. Grim determination flashed from the eyes of each horseman as the band thundered toward the complacent dwelling of Nabal.

It was then that Abigail, the peacemaker, wise and beautiful wife of Nabal, gathered up provisions and went forth to meet the angry young men of the desert. Bowing to the ground before David, she begged, "Receive this blessing, which your handmaid has brought to you, my lord, and give it to the young men that follow you. Forgive the iniquity of your handmaid, for the Lord will surely make for you a faithful house, because you, my lord, fight His battles; let not evil therefore be found in you all the days of your life."

And the angry young warrior was appeased and blessed God for having averted the slaughter. "Blessed be you," he exclaimed, "who have kept me from coming to blood!"

Abigail returned home content, having left history a concrete example of the beatitude: "Blessed are the peacemakers, for they shall be called the children of God" (Matthew 5:9).

—1 Samuel 25

7. Women of the Bible (O.T.)

THE STOLEN EWE

Nathan the prophet took a deep breath. He had no relish for what he was about to say. Before him sat King David, once called from the pastures of Bethlehem by the Lord Himself to shepherd all Israel in God's name. And now Nathan must tell the king that the Lord was sorely displeased.

"There were two men in one city," the prophet began, "the one rich, and the other poor. The rich man had a great many sheep and oxen. But the poor man had nothing at all but one little ewe lamb, which he had bought and nourished, and which had grown up in his house together with his children, eating of his bread and drinking of his cup, and sleeping in his bosom; and it was like a daughter to him.

BATHSHEBA — THE STOLEN EWE BATHSHEBA — THE STOLEN EWE BATHSH

And when a certain stranger came to visit the rich man, he spared to take of his own sheep and oxen to make a feast for that stranger, but took the poor man's ewe, and dressed it for the man who had come to visit him."

Angry, King David demanded the name of the man who had done this terrible thing. "He shall restore the ewe fourfold, because he did this thing and had no pity!"

"You are the man," the prophet replied. "Thus says the Lord...'You have killed Uria the Hittite with the sword and have taken his wife (Bathsheba) to be your wife.... Behold, I will raise up evil against you out of your own house!"

"I have sinned against the Lord!" the king cried out in sorrow. And God, who reads men's hearts, inspired Nathan to reply, "The Lord has taken away your sin."

But the penance remained to be done. David's weeping and fasting and his composition of the most famous penitential psalm, the *Miserere,* were but a portion of his expiation. One of the king's own sons rose up in rebellion against him and drove him into exile. King David took it from the hands of God, and eventually the kingdom was restored to him.

Even though strong temptations may overcome those who are loyal to God, true sorrow and a spirit of penance "He will not reject."

—2 Samuel 11 and 12

The Miserere

Have mercy on me, O God, in your goodness;
in the greatness of your compassion
wipe out my offense.
Thoroughly wash me from my guilt
and of my sin cleanse me....

A clean heart create for me, O God,
and a steadfast spirit renew within me.
Cast me not out from your presence,
and your holy spirit take not from me.
Give me back the joy of your salvation
and a willing spirit sustain in me.
I will teach transgressors your ways,
and sinners shall return to you.
Free me from blood guilt,
O God, my saving God;
then my tongue shall revel
in your justice.
O Lord, open my lips,
and my mouth shall proclaim your praise.
For you are not pleased with sacrifices;
should I offer a holocaust,
you would not accept it.
My sacrifice, O God,
is a contrite spirit;
a heart contrite and humbled,
O God, you will not spurn.

—Psalm 50

THE QUEEN OF SABA

SHE CAME TO HEAR WISDOM

It was night. Solomon, son of Bathsheba, slept peacefully, for the kingdom he had half-inherited from his father, half-wrested from his brother, was safe at last. The young king began to dream of the God of his father David, whom he, too, loved sincerely. "Ask what you wish I should give you," said the Lord in the dream.

Solomon did not hesitate. "Give your servant an understanding heart to judge your people and discern between good and evil. For who can worthily judge these people of yours, who are so numerous?"

"Because this choice has pleased your heart," replied the Lord, "and you have not asked wealth and glory, nor the lives of those who hate you, nor many days of life, but have asked wisdom and knowl-

edge, to be able to judge my people, over which I have made you king, wisdom and knowledge are granted to you. And I will give you such riches and glory that none of the kings before you or after you shall be like you."

And so it was. The reign of Solomon was blessed with such wisdom, peace and prosperity that the boundaries of his realm spread farther and farther; kingdom became empire. Farther still radiated Solomon's reputation.

The queen of Saba decided to come and see for herself. Hers was a prosperous nation, the modern Yemen, located in southern Arabia. Sabean caravans trekked up and down the great trade route between Asia Minor and the Far East. The little kingdom was famous for its gold, spices, frankincense and precious stones.

"The queen of Saba, having heard of the fame of Solomon, came to try him with hard questions. And entering into Jerusalem with a great train, and riches, and camels that carried spices, and an immense quantity of gold, and precious stones, she came to King Solomon, and spoke to him all that she had in her heart."

To the queen's surprise, there was no question that the king could not answer, no riddle that he could not solve. Moreover, she was amazed at Solomon's wealth and power—his splendid palace and savory foods, the order and garb of his ministers, and especially the magnificent temple that the king had erected for divine worship.

"The word is true," she exclaimed to Solomon, "which I heard in my country of your virtues and wisdom. I did not believe those who told it, until I came, and my eyes had seen, and I had proved that hardly half of your wisdom had been told me.... Happy are your men, and happy are your servants, who stand always before you, and hear your wisdom. Blessed be the Lord your God, who has been pleased to set you on his throne.... Because God loves Israel, and will preserve them forever: therefore he has made you king over them, to do judgment and justice."

She gave King Solomon an abundance of spices, gold and precious stones: "There were no such spices as these which the queen of Saba gave to King Solomon."

Years later, when inspiring one of His prophets to foretell the glory of the new Sion, the Lord clothed His message in the imagery of Israel's golden age: "You shall be radiant at what you see, your heart shall throb and overflow, for the riches of the sea shall be emptied out before you, the wealth of nations shall be brought to you. Caravans of camels shall fill you, dromedaries from Madian and Epha; all from Saba shall come, bearing gold and frankincense and proclaiming the praises of the Lord" (Isaia 60:5-6).

Laden with gifts, the queen of Saba returned to her homeland. Her pilgrimage had not gone unnoticed by the Lord. A thousand years later, Jesus was to say: "The queen of the South will rise up in judgment with this generation and will condemn it; for she came from the ends of the earth to hear the wisdom of Solomon..." (Matthew 12:42).

The queen of Saba shows us the value of wisdom, a quality especially important in our own times. "Our era needs wisdom more than bygone ages if the discoveries made by men are to be further humanized," the Second Vatican Council told us. "The future of the world stands in peril unless wiser men are forthcoming" (Church in the Modern World).

—3 Kings 3 to 10

Praise of Wisdom

All wisdom comes from the Lord
and with him it remains forever.
The sand of the seashore,
the drops of rain,
the days of eternity:
who can number these?
Heaven's height,
earth's breadth,
the depths of the abyss:
who can explore these?
Before all things else
Wisdom was created;
and prudent understanding
from eternity.
To whom has wisdom's root been revealed?
Who knows her subtleties?
There is but one,
wise and truly awe-inspiring,
seated upon his throne:
It is the Lord;
he created her,
has seen her
and taken note of her.
He has poured her forth
upon all his works,
upon every living thing

according to his bounty;
he has lavished her upon his friends.

Fear of the Lord is glory and splendor,
gladness and a festive crown.
Fear of the Lord warms the heart,
giving gladness and joy and length of days.
He who fears the Lord
will have a happy end;
even on the day of his death
he will be blessed.
The beginning of wisdom is the fear of the Lord,
which is formed with the faithful in the womb.
With devoted men was she created from of old,
and with her children her beneficence abides.
Fullness of wisdom is fear of the Lord;
she inebriates men with her fruits.
Her entire house she fills with choice foods,
her granaries with her harvest.
Wisdom's garland is fear of the Lord,
with blossoms of peace and perfect health.
Knowledge and full understanding she showers down;
she heightens the glory of those who possess her.
The root of wisdom is fear of the Lord;
her branches are length of days.

—Sirach 1

THE WOMAN OF SUNAM

HER FAITH WAS REWARDED

She lived in a peaceful village on the northern rim of the Valley of Esdraelon, on the border of what would one day be southern Galilee. Although her family was wealthy, riches had brought little joy into her life, for she had no son and her husband was advanced in years.

Frequently the prophet Eliseus would stop in to accept her traditional oriental hospitality. The devout woman was pleased to be of service to such a holy man of God, successor of the famed Elia who on neighboring Mount Carmel had called fire down from heaven to consume a holocaust in proof of Yahweh's power. Rumor had it that Eliseus had asked Elia to obtain twice as much prophetical spirit for him, and that the Lord had indeed granted this favor after Elia's passing.

One day the good woman of Sunam exclaimed to her husband, "This prophet who stops by so often is a sacred man of God. Let us build him a little room and put a little bed in it for him, and a table and a stool and a candlestick, so that when he stops in, he may stay there." And so it was done. Often such rooms were simple huts of leafy branches; this chamber, instead, was walled. It was located, in utter privacy, on the roof terrace. The furnishings were a further mark of respect, for poor people in Palestine sat and slept on the floor.

The man of God was fully aware of the respect shown him by the well-to-do couple. One day, as he was resting in the roof chamber, he told his servant, Giezi, to ask the Sunamitess if he could do her any favor, such as speak to the king or the general in behalf of her interests. She replied, through the servant, that there was no need. "What, then, will she have me do for her?" Eliseus asked his servant.

"Do not ask," replied Giezi, "for she has no son, and her husband is old."

The prophet then promised the woman a son in a year's time. And to her great joy, the promise came true.

The boy grew. One day he went into the fields with his father to see how the reapers were progressing with the harvest. The sunlight was unusually strong. "My head, my head," the boy began to moan.

"Take him to his mother," the father told a servant.

It was sunstroke. The poor mother did everything she could, but it was too late. The boy whom Eliseus had asked of God died in his mother's arms.

Resolutely the Sunamitess carried the child up to the prophet's empty chamber and laid him on the bed. Then she sought out her husband. "Please let me take one of the servants and a donkey," she said. "I want to pay a call on the man of God."

The Sunamite looked at his wife in surprise. It was neither new moon, nor sabbath; this was not the right time for a pilgrimage. But she was determined and would say no more, so he let her go.

From his dwelling on the slopes of Mount Carmel, Eliseus saw her coming. Out of politeness, he sent Giezi to meet her and ask if all were well with herself and her family. It was a conventional greeting, to which the woman replied briefly and evasively, "Well." She was determined to speak to the prophet directly.

"And when she came to the man of God on the mount, she caught hold of his feet, and Giezi came to remove her. And the man of God said: 'Let her alone, for her soul is in anguish. The Lord has hidden this from me and has not told me.' "

Sending Giezi on ahead, the prophet hastened with the distraught mother to Sunam. "And going in he shut the door upon him, and upon the child, and prayed to the Lord. And he went up, and lay upon the child; and he put his mouth upon his mouth, and his eyes upon his eyes, and his hands upon his hands; and he bowed himself upon him, and the child's flesh grew warm. Then he returned and walked in the house, once to and fro; and he went up, and lay upon him, and the child sneezed seven times and opened his eyes. And he called Giezi, and said to him: Call this Sunamitess. And she being called, went in to him, and he said: 'Take up your son.'"

The woman's gratitude was admirable. Before turning to the boy, she bowed in homage before the man of God. Then she took up the child who had been restored to her by God's power in answer to her faith.

—4 Kings 4

A Woman of Virtue

Happy the husband of a good wife,
twice lengthened are his days;
a worthy wife brings joy to her husband,
peaceful and full is his life.
A good wife is a generous gift
bestowed upon him who fears the Lord;
be he rich or poor,
his heart is content,
and a smile is ever on his face....

A gracious wife delights her husband,
her thoughtfulness puts flesh on his bones;
a gift from the Lord is her governed speech,
and her firm virtue is of surpassing worth.
Choicest of blessings is a modest wife,
priceless her chaste person.
Like the sun rising in the Lord's heavens,
the beauty of a virtuous wife
is the radiance of her home. —Sirach 26

AN HEROIC MOTHER

HER COURAGE NEVER FAILED

During the fierce religious persecution from which Judas Machabeus and his brothers struggled to deliver the Hebrew people, men, women and children suffered martyrdom rather than deny their Faith. The heroic story of a certain mother and her seven sons is one of the most moving narrations in all of Scripture.

This brave family was led before the pagan ruler, King Antiochus, and ordered to disobey a religious prescription that had been handed down for generations.

Courageously, the eldest son replied, "We are ready to die rather than transgress the laws of God, received from our fathers." Upon hearing this, his captors tortured him horribly until he died. Meanwhile his brothers and mother urged one another to die with courage.

When the second brother was at the point of death after suffering similar torments, he exclaimed to the tyrant, "You indeed destroy us out of the present life, but the King of the world will raise us, who die for his laws, in the resurrection of eternal life."

As he stretched out his hands for the torture, the third brother exclaimed, "These I have from heaven, but for the laws of God I now despise them, because I hope to receive them again from him."

As they went to their martyrdom, the mother exhorted her sons one by one. "I do not know how you were formed in my womb," she said, "for I neither gave you breath, nor soul, nor life, neither did I frame the limbs of any one of you. But the Creator of the world...will restore to you again in his mercy both breath and life, as now you despise yourselves for the sake of his laws."

When only the youngest boy remained, King Antiochus turned to the mother and urged her to coax him to yield and save his life.

"Yes, I will counsel my son," she replied. But she did not tell the king what she intended to say. Bending over the boy, she said in their own language, "I beg you, my son, look upon heaven and earth, and all that is in them, and consider that God made them out of nothing, and mankind also. So you shall not fear this tormentor, but being made a worthy partner with your brothers, receive death, that in that mercy I may receive you again with your brothers."

Turning to King Antiochus, the boy declared, "I will not obey the commandment of the king, but the commandment of the law, which was given us by Moses.... My brothers, who have now undergone a brief pain, are under the covenant of eternal life; but you by the judgment of God shall receive just punishment for your pride. As did my brothers, I offer up my life and my body for the laws of our fathers, calling upon God to be speedily merciful to our nation, and that you by torments and stripes may confess that he alone is God...."

Thus, the last son and the courageous mother died amid the same cruel torments, trusting the God who made them would raise them up on the last day. "The hour is coming," Jesus was to say, "when all who are in the tombs shall hear the voice of the Son of God. And they who have done good shall come forth unto resurrection of life; but they who have done evil unto resurrection of judgment" (John 5:28-29).

—2 Machabees 7

The Final Triumph

Then shall the just one with great assurance
stand before his oppressors
who set at nought his labors.
Seeing this, they shall be shaken with dreadful fear,
and amazed at the unlooked-for salvation.
They shall say among themselves,
rueful and groaning through anguish of spirit:
"This is he whom we once held as a laughingstock
and as a type for mockery,
fools that we were!
His life we deemed madness,
and his death dishonored.
See how he is accounted among the sons of God;
how his lot is with the saints!...

What did our pride avail us?
What have wealth and its boastfulness afforded us?
All of them passed like a shadow
and like a fleeting rumor;..."

Yes, the hope of the wicked
is like thistledown borne on the wind,
and like fine, tempest-driven foam;
like smoke scattered by the wind,
and like the passing memory of the nomad
camping for a single day.
But the just live forever,
and in the Lord is their recompense,
and the thought of them
is with the Most High.
Therefore shall they receive the splendid crown,
the beauteous diadem,
from the hand of the Lord....

—Wisdom 5

Daughters of St. Paul

In Massachusetts
50 St. Paul's Avenue, *Boston,* Mass. 02130
172 Tremont Street, *Boston,* Mass. 02111
In New York
78 Fort Place, *Staten Island,* N.Y. 10301
625 East 187th Street, *Bronx,* N.Y. 10458
525 Main Street, *Buffalo,* N.Y. 14203
In Connecticut
202 Fairfield Avenue, *Bridgeport,* Conn. 06603
In Ohio
415 Euclid Avenue, *Cleveland,* Ohio 44114
In Pennsylvania
1127 South Broad Street, *Philadelphia,* Pa. 19147
In Florida
2700 Biscayne Blvd., *Miami,* Florida 33137
In Louisiana
4403 Veterans Memorial Blvd., *Metairie,* La. 70002
86 Bolton Avenue, *Alexandria,* La. 71301
In Texas
114 East Main Plaza, *San Antonio,* Texas 78205
In California
1570 Fifth Avenue, *San Diego,* Calif. 92101
278 17th Street, *Oakland,* Calif. 94612
587 Market Street, near 2nd Street, *San Francisco,* Calif. 94105
In Canada
3022 Dufferin Street, *Toronto* 395, Ontario, Canada
In England
57, Kensington Church Street, *London* W. 8, England
In Australia
58, Abbotsford Rd., Homebush, N.S.W., *Sydney* 2140, Australia
In Philippine Islands
2650, F.B. Harrison, P.O. Box 3576, *Pasay City,* Manila, Philippine Islands
In India
143, Waterfield Road, Bandra, *Bombay,* 50-AS, India
In Africa
35, Jones Street, P.O. Box 3243, *Lagos,* Nigeria